AF530887

DRIED FLOWERS

How to Prepare Them

BY SARAH WHITLOCK
AND MARTHA RANKIN

DOVER PUBLICATIONS, INC.
New York

Published in Canada by General Publishing Company, Ltd., 30 Lesmill Road, Don Mills, Toronto, Ontario.
Published in the United Kingdom by Constable and Company, Ltd., 10 Orange Street, London WC 2.

This Dover edition, first published in 1975, is a republication of the work first published in 1962 under the title *New Techniques with Dried Flowers*. It is reprinted by special arrangement with the original publisher, Hearthside Press, Inc., 445 Northern Boulevard, Great Neck, New York 11021.

International Standard Book Number: 0-486-21802-3
Library of Congress Catalog Card Number: 75-17126

Manufactured in the United States of America
Dover Publications, Inc.
180 Varick Street
New York, N.Y. 10014

TABLE OF CONTENTS

introduction

Lovely flowers, dried in rich vibrant colors that harmonize with their setting, are a delight not only during the winter months, but at other seasons and occasions. When our gardens do not have materials in the desired colors, or when we are too busy to cut and arrange fresh designs, the dried arrangement is a real blessing. For those who have no cutting garden of their own, flowers picked from roadside (provided they are not on the conservation list in your state!) or bought at the florist, may be dried and enjoyed for months.

In making dried arrangements we are not restricted, as with fresh flowers, to whatever is blooming at the time, because if we start collecting in early spring and continue until late fall, we assemble a great wealth of beautiful dried materials from beginning to end of the entire growing season. Thus we have not only many colors, but every shape and form of flower; round, spiky, or branching; single flowers, clusters and floreted blossoms. In addition, there will be berries, seed pods, grasses, and foliage. As every flower arranger knows, very artistic and beautiful results may be obtained from such a variety of materials.

We know that for generations flowers have been dried for winter decoration and that various methods have been used. We have tried them all. We learned of *hanging* them and of preserving them in either *borax* or *sand*. The flowers that could be dried successfully by *hanging* were lovely, but we were not satisfied with the use of borax as it caked badly, and we found the sand too heavy.

We determined, therefore, to find some medium that would be so *light* and *fluffy* that even the most delicate flower could be dried without tearing the petals. In 1949 we began experimenting with everything imaginable, from flour to vermiculite.

Finally, we tried white corn meal. We found to our delight that the flowers were drying perfectly. But after leaving them another week to complete the drying, we looked and alas, there were no flowers as the weevils had had a banquet! By adding borax to the corn meal, we solved our problem. There were no more weevils, and we found that the mixture could be used over and over, year after year, provided it is kept perfectly dry.

We were encouraged in our experiments by the need for eighteenth century floral decorations for Monticello, Thomas Jefferson's historic home. We had the satisfaction of helping our garden club maintain some sixteen different dried arrangements in the stately old rooms throughout several winters.

In the summer of 1961 a new agent for drying flowers was introduced. This is silica gel, a chemical compound which readily absorbs moisture. Almost all flowers dried in silica gel retain their brightness of color and beauty of form. In addition, it has the advantage of acting very fast. Having made a thorough study of this material, we have made many recommendations throughout our book for its use.

what and when to collect

Collecting flowers for drying draws attention to many beauties of nature that might otherwise be overlooked. The collector should not wait till summer, with its profusion of blooms, but must be ready to observe and select from springtime's earliest offerings of pussy willow and daffodil.

The flower garden, of course, will supply choice specimens throughout the growing season until frost takes the last little chrysanthemum. But beyond the garden gate this delightful hobby leads you into fields and woods in search of decorative shapes, colors, and textures. The lowly milkweed's pod is lined with gold and sumac's torch of crimson berries may be just the right accent needed for striking dried arrangements. In the foliage and berries of autumn you will find that there is much color to be harvested. A profusion of lovely materials for drying, both flowers and foliage, is to be found in the florist shops at all seasons of the year.

The hobby of drying flowers enhances the discoveries of traveling. A collector scans new scenes more closely for unusual materials not obtainable at home. Such non-perishable oddities as tornillo pods or cotton pods are brought back from a trip for a double purpose; they give novelty to dried arrangements and serve as mementos too.

methods of drying

Flowers and foliage must be dried separately and by different methods.

Small compact blooms usually dry well by the old-fashioned technique of hanging. Flowers with large or intricately shaped petals, or heads that must be supported in place during drying, need the silica gel, meal and borax, perlite or sand and borax treatment.

For foliage too, there is a choice of methods. Leaves pressed between weighted newspapers or magazines will keep their coloring of either summer green or autumnal red and yellow, but will dry flat and brittle. Another process of treating leaves is with glycerin and water, one that will preserve both flexibility and three-dimensional arrangement but usually at the sacrifice of color stability.

Grasses can be dried standing upright in a container, thereby bending in a natural curve, or they may be hung by the stems in a bunch.

Choose the method that promises best results for the material that you have chosen.

1. Hanging Method

Many flowers dry well by this extremely simple process. If you are too busy, or lack space for other methods, you can easily hang them and still have lovely material for winter bouquets. Flowers used in the beautiful arrangements in the exhibition buildings of Colonial Williamsburg are all dried in this manner and are in keeping with the custom practiced in that era.

See reference list on page 22 for flowers that dry well by hanging.

Tie flowers in loose bunches and hang heads down until they are dry. Space is saved by using a wire coat hanger from which several bunches of flowers may be suspended. To tie and hang the flowers easily, wind an elastic band several times around the stems, loop it over the wire of the hanger and catch it again in ends of the stems. The bunches can be removed easily with a slight jerk or pull.

2. Surrounding and Covering Method

This is a more complicated method in which flower heads are *surrounded* and *covered* by a medium that holds the petals and other parts of the flower in place during dehydration. For this purpose there is a choice of materials that may be used. These are silica gel, meal and borax, perlite, and sand and borax.

The most perfect results are obtained with the silica gel; however, there are the other mediums that may be used. We have found that meal and borax are very satisfactory and dry all flowers extremely well. Perlite, or sand and borax, also bring good results.

The general principle of dehydration is the same no matter which of the mediums you choose to use, but the silica gel must be handled quite differently as its affinity for moisture makes it imperative that it be kept in an airtight container *at all times.*

preparing the flowers

All flowers, unless otherwise noted, should be cut when they first come into full bloom. It is safest, of course, to dry them immediately but if this is not convenient and they have been well conditioned, it will do no harm to delay dehydration for a short time. To condition, place flowers in deep, slightly tepid water overnight or for at least five or six hours.

If drying must be delayed for several days, flowers should be kept in the refrigerator. In extreme cases it will often be possible to keep them fresh for a much longer period by means of the following method. Make sure that there is no dew or other moisture on any part of the flower. Immediately after cutting put the flowers in a large plastic bag and twist the end, secure it with an elastic band to be certain that it is made airtight and place the bag in the refrigerator. The flowers will then remain fresh for as long as two weeks without ever having been in water. After removing these from the refrigerator recut ends of stems diagonally and condition the flowers in warm water. This no doubt sounds fantastic but try it and see!

When gathering flowers or other plant material any distance from home, place them in a small amount of water (exception: glycerin-treated leaves) to keep fresh in transit. If this is not possible and you find that they have wilted somewhat before you reach home, they may very often be revived as follows; flowers such as peonies, roses, dogwood, chrysanthemums and others that have hard or woody stems should be put in hot water in a metal container and left until the water has cooled. First recut the stem ends and crush slightly. Flowers with soft stems, daffodils, for instance, should be put in warm water because they cannot take much heat.

Before drying, be sure to remove, or dry thoroughly, the wet part of the stem. Also see that there is no moisture on any part of the flower. Strip all foliage from flowers that are to be dried.

substitute stems

When drying flowers that have no stems of their own, such as hollyhocks that are pinched from the stalk as blossoms bloom and strawflowers that are usually picked very close to the head, a substitute stem must be made before drying. Insert a piece of florist wire into the back of the flower. During dehydration the flower will shrink around the wire, holding it firmly in place. We also add stems to any flowers that require it, after they have dried. See page 31 for technique.

where to dry

A dry, dark, warm place should be used for the drying. Attics, closets or hot furnace rooms are ideal but never a garage or an ordinary basement because of the dampness.

silica gel, sensational development

This new chemical compound is expensive, and rather difficult to work with, but the results well merit its use. Exceptionally beautiful are roses, camellias, delphiniums, dahlias, Christmas roses, and daffodils preserved in gel. After continual tests, we are convinced that it is the best of all materials for drying flowers. However, let us assure you that if your time is limited, or your pocketbook slim, you must *not* feel that it is a necessity. The other mediums have much to offer; we have been using them for years and know that they will enable you to dry all of the lovely flowers that you could wish. If you decide to invest in silica gel, you should have a minimum of five pounds, but ten or fifteen are preferable. This will be costly but once you have purchased a supply it will last always. We feel that it is impractical to use silica gel for foliage when the other mediums will do just as well, and other methods (glycerin and pressing) are much easier and often better. We advise, in most cases, using silica gel for flowers only. You will find on pages 21 through 27, a list of flowers for which we particularly recommend it.

the different mediums

A. SILICA GEL

Silica gel has many industrial uses, among which are the packaging of baby powders and certain foods such as potato chips and cereals. It is also now being prepared especially for drying flowers and is sold under brand names at garden shops, hardware, chain and drug stores, and by mail order.

These preparations are composed of a combination of two sizes of the gel, a fine mesh that is white and a small amount of a coarser mesh that is blue. When the blue "Tel-Tale" fades to white or turns pink it is an indication that it has absorbed moisture and cannot be used again until it has been reactivated. This is done by placing it in a shallow pan in the oven at 300 degrees F. until the blue color returns. It should then immediately be poured into an airtight container and allowed to cool before reusing. Silica gel may be used over and over again.

Mixing your own silica gel compound is not very practical. It is more expensive than the ready mixed preparations and also the materials are not always available in small quantities. If for some reason, however, you do prefer to make your own mix, here is the formula that we advise:

Mix thoroughly ⅓ lb. of 6-16 mesh silica gel (Tel-Tale) with 5 lbs. of 28-200 mesh.

An interesting feature about silica gel and one that you should know is that it could actually be soaking wet, yet to the touch and all outward appearances it will seem to be "bone dry." For this reason the "Tel-Tale" blue, or indicating grain, is absolutely necessary to let you know by its color when the gel must be dried out in the oven.

B. MEAL AND BORAX

Combine ten parts of white cornmeal with three parts borax and mix thoroughly. (If some of this adheres to flowers after drying, it may be shaken off or removed with a small paintbrush.)

C. PERLITE AGGREGATE (crushed volcanic rock)

This is used in mixing plaster and can be obtained at building supply houses. It is fast acting and very inexpensive.

D. SAND AND BORAX

If white corn meal is not available in your vicinity, sand may be used in its place, washed and sifted if necessary. We prefer meal and borax but when sand is lightened with borax in proportions according to weight of the sand you will find it efficient. Heavy sand needs three fourths borax to one fourth sand, whereas a fine sand requires only one fourth borax to three fourths sand.

After you have chosen the medium that you wish to use, the next step is to decide whether the flowers should be dried *face-up* (example, peonies), *face-down* (gloriosa daisies), or horizontally (spike of delphinium).

drying flowers face-up

Many flowers dry best *face-up,* their stems hanging straight down. To accomplish this we give the following directions.

SILICA GEL (FACE-UP)

Obtain a 50 lb. lard tin from your hardware store. Cut a strip of corrugated cardboard seven or eight inches wide to fit inside and around the lower part. Place on top of this a circular piece of two-inch Styrofoam that has been cut one fourth of an inch *smaller* than circumference of the can.

In order that this may be easily removed make a handle by inserting a folded piece of rather heavy florist wire through the center, leaving a three-inch loop for the handle on top and bending the underneath wires at right angles to make secure.

Honeycomb the Styrofoam with an ice pick, or other similar object, so that when stems of flowers are put through they will hang straight down while the heads are supported and will remain on top.

To prevent the silica gel from trickling through the holes when flowers are being covered, place on top of the Styrofoam a

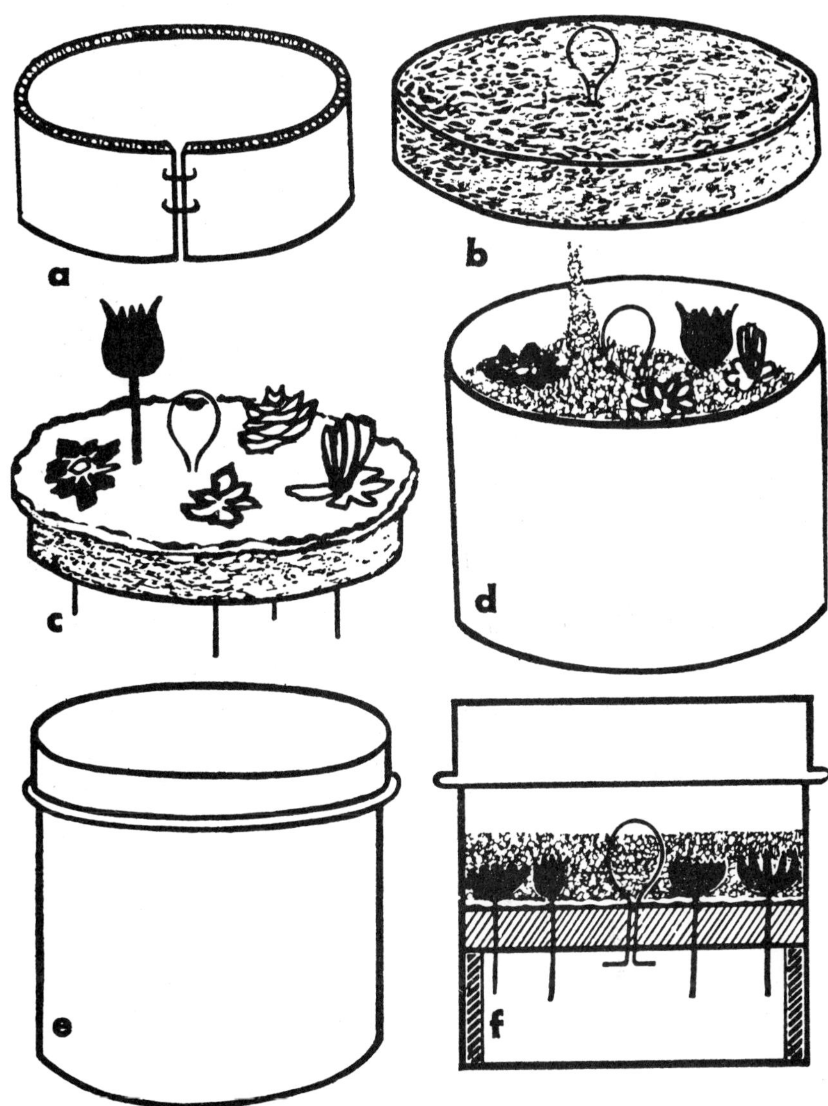

Drying flowers face-up in silica gel. a) Cardboard ends are stapled together; b) a handle of heavy florist wire is made in the styrofoam; c) stems are inserted through styrofoam and a thin layer of cotton; d) silica gel is gently poured around and over flowers; e) be sure lid fits tightly, or seal with tape; f) a cross-section view showing cardboard, styrofoam, cotton, stems, and silica gel.

thin piece of cotton, either absorbent or batting, that has been cut one inch wider than the Styrofoam.

Now you are ready to put flowers into the can. To do this, lift the cotton slightly to find where the holes have been pierced and draw stems of the flowers through both the cotton and the Styrofoam. Be sure that the cotton is well around the stems and that the heads of the flowers left on top are not touching. Gently pour the silica gel under, around and between the petals until the flowers are lightly but completely covered. Take great care not to bend or disarrange any part of the flower and last, but not least, be very certain that the tightly fitted lid is firmly pressed on the can immediately.

You will find that when this medium is used the stems do not always dry as quickly as the heads of the flowers, therefore it is wise to hang them until they are thoroughly dry, before using.

If you wish to dry a few flowers only, ones with very short stems, a cake or candy tin or other sealable container may be used. If you place a one-inch piece of Styrofoam, cut to fit, in the bottom of the can it will save a great deal of silica gel. The stems may then be inserted and covered as directed above. If container is not perfectly tight, seal the lid with freezer tape.

When sufficient time has been allowed for dehydration, carefully pour off and save the silica gel, and remove flowers from the Styrofoam.

OTHER MEDIUMS (FACE-UP)

Use a heavy cardboard or corrugated box about three inches in depth propped over a carton eight or more inches high. Punch holes in the shallow box far enough apart for heads of the flowers not to touch and large enough for the stems to go through. Proceed in the same manner as that described for covering with silica gel, only it is not necessary to cover the box.

drying flowers face-down or horizontally

ALL MEDIUMS

If flowers are to be dried *face-down,* or *horizontally,* cover bottom of the can or box with an inch or more of the medium you have chosen. Holding the flower slightly above this, lightly fluff it up, under, around and over until the flower is barely covered. Put only one layer in each can or box. Clusters of flowers may also be dried in this way. Stems need not be covered.

time required for drying

The time needed for dehydration depends upon a number of things; temperature, humidity, medium used and moisture content of the flower. A marigold, for instance, will take as long as three weeks while a hollyhock will take only a few days. All flowers in silica gel dry more quickly than in other mediums. A sure test of their dryness is to brush aside a little of the medium and if the petals are crisp to the touch they will be thoroughly dry. If the hanging method is used the testing is simple.

additional heat for quick drying

It is sometimes desirable to hasten the drying time of certain flowers. This may be accomplished by placing the box, or can, containing the flowers, on top of a furnace. Watch the flowers carefully and remove from the heat as soon as they are dry, or they will become too brittle. Any flower desired in a hurry may be dried in this way.

If you use the hanging method and desire quick drying, suspend flowers directly over the furnace.

combining fresh and dried material

Sometimes, to give an extremely naturalistic effect, dried flowers may be used with fresh evergreen foliage. If well conditioned, all foliage of this type will last for several weeks so that the arrangement will be semi-permanent. To condition, crush ends of the stems an inch or more and submerge the entire branch ten to twelve hours. When the foliage fades it will be a simple matter to replace with fresh evergreens. Hemlock seems to be a misunderstood evergreen. Frequently it has appeared in print that the needles are inclined to drop, making it impractical to use in arrangements. Our opinion is that when this happens the hemlock has not been *thoroughly conditioned.* If treated as directed above and always kept in water we have found, after having used it for nearly two years in arrangements, that it will definitely last for at least two weeks. Possibly, if kept in an extremely hot and very dry room, the needles might drop, but under normal conditions it is long-lasting and dependable.

In making the arrangement be certain that the stems of the dried flowers do not touch the water in the container. In order to accomplish this attach a florist pick to the end of the stem.

Another suggestion which we highly recommend is the combination of dried pussy willows with fresh daffodils or other flowers. The season for pussy willows being so short we think that it is very advantageous to dry them, after which one can scarcely distinguish them from those freshly cut.

foliage

As dried flowers have been stripped of their own leaves it is important that other foliage be dried to use with them. All kinds of leaves may be used. Green leaves and ferns may be gathered at any time *after* the new growth has hardened; brilliantly colored fall foliage should be cut as soon as possible after color has changed.

Nearly all small-leaved foliage can be dried in three dimensions by using the *S & C* method. They will be brittle but attractive when used in arrangements.

drying foliage by pressing

Ferns, Dusty Miller and small leaves that are flat on their branches (example, privet) are quite useful. These are easily dried between pages of magazines. Larger branches of foliage should be placed on a thick layer of newspaper with care that leaves do not overlap. Cover with several layers of paper and repeat until all are covered, but do not have too large a pile. Press with boards, or similar flat objects, and heavily weight the entire pile. They may also be put under a heavy rug.

Allow about three weeks for drying. Green leaves will retain their color and autumn leaves will remain red or yellow as they were originally.

glycerin for drying foliage in three dimensions

We consider native beech leaves that have been treated in glycerin (which you can buy at the drug store) to be the loveliest and most useful of all foliage material. Cut them when green, or after they have turned a golden yellow in the fall. Crush the stems about two inches and let stand in a deep container, filled with a solution of one third glycerin to two thirds water for thirty-six hours after which they should be removed and stored in a dark place until ready for use. The green leaves will have acquired a slightly olive cast but otherwise will remain flexible and exactly as when cut. Branches of red barberry will also keep their shape and color when treated in this manner.

Green beech leaves that have been exposed to light for several weeks will begin to turn slightly tan. It is therefore wise to provide an extra supply for replacement.

Many other leaves will dry successfully in the glycerin and water (examples; magnolia, forsythia, boxwood, rhododendron, etc.); nearly all of them will turn brown but will be soft and lovely. This process will require about three weeks, and the solution should be replenished as it evaporates. All foliage to be treated in the glycerin *must* be put in the solution *immediately, never plain water* as it should start absorbing glycerin at once.

If ivy leaves and stems are submerged in the glycerin solution and left for four days, they will be a lovely shade of green and may be used with fruits or vegetables as a centerpiece. As soon as removed rinse the glycerin off with cool water.

key to decorator colors

Although the color of most flowers remains about the same after drying, the shades of the colors often vary. Sometimes they will turn lighter, but frequently they will deepen. Occasionally the color itself changes. A cerise zinnia, for instance, turns purple, a royal purple larkspur becomes almost a true blue, and a bright yellow corcopsis will change to a beautiful orange.

A color which seldom dries successfully is bright red or scarlet. We usually depend for red upon autumn foliage, such as sumac and maple, or berries. Sometimes light yellowish red zinnias will turn to an attractive bright red in *silica gel.*

Do not attempt to dry shaded flowers, or those of bronze and rust hues, as they turn a rather muddy and unattractive color.

Some varieties of the same flower dry better than others as to color. This is particularly noticeable in yellow marigolds. The lovely "Glitters" will not turn out to be a pretty dried flower, but the tiny "Lemon Drop" and several of the larger varieties dry beautifully. Do experiment with the different varieties that you grow.

most satisfactory material in various colors

CRIMSON:	Hollyhocks, roses, strawflowers, cockscomb.
ROSE and PINK:	Peonies, hollyhocks, roses, strawflowers, larkspur, delphinium, zinnias, cockscomb, globe amaranth.
RED:	Bittersweet, nandina, and other berries. Chinese lantern pods. Fall foliage, especially maple and sumac. DARK RED: Strawflowers.

ORANGE: Marigolds, strawflowers, Mexican sunflowers, zinnias.

YELLOW: Yarrow, statice, zinnias, chrysanthemums, marigolds, goldenrod, strawflowers, daffodils.

GREEN: Sprays of caryopteris pods, hydrangea flowers, globe thistle buds, ferns and foliage.

BLUE: Larkspur, delphinium, blue hydrangea, salvia.

LAVENDER: Statice, xeranthemums, larkspur, delphiniums.

WHITE: Statice, baby's breath, larkspur, delphiniums, Christmas roses, strawflowers, Queen Anne's lace, pearly everlasting, honesty, dahlias, Japanese anemones.

REFERENCE LIST OF MATERIALS AND METHODS

The following flowers are those which to our knowledge dry well. There will be many other satisfactory flowers in different localities. You not only will find pleasure in experimenting for yourselves but will doubtless make some interesting discoveries.

key to abbreviations

H. Hanging method, see page 9.

S & C. Surrounding and covering method, see page 10 (includes all mediums). If silica gel is especially recommended for any particular flower, this will be noted.

R. Recommended variety.

flowers

Acacia: Tree. Dries easily and beautifully. S & C. Face down. Silica gel recommended but other mediums do well.

Acrolinium: Annual. H. Pick in bud.

Anemone Japonica: Perennial. S & C. Face up.

Baby's Breath: Perennial. H. Easily dried and very useful. R: "Bristol Fairy."

Bells of Ireland: Annual. H. Holds shape best if cut after most of the small white flowers in center of bells have bloomed. Must be put in arrangements early in fall or bells will drop.

Black-eyed Susan: Field flower. S & C. Face down.

Blue Sage: [Salvia] Annual. H. Cut in fall when color is deepest. R: "Bluo Farinacea."

Butterfly Bush: [Buddleia] S & C. Horizontal.

Camellia: Shrub. S & C. Face up.

Chives: Perennial herb. H. Silver-lavender flowers.

Chrysanthemum: Perennial. H. or S & C. Clear yellow dries best. Some pinks and white good. R: "Charles Nye." Face up or down.

Christmas Rose: [Helleborus niger] Perennial. S & C. Silica gel recommended. Face up.

Clematis: Vine. S & C. R: "Lawsonia" or "Ramona" or "Paniculata." Face up.

Cockscomb: [Celosia] Annual. H. Crimson, rose, and pink. Crested or plumed. R: "Gilbert's Rose Beauty," "Harlequin," "Toredor," "Pride of Castle Gould," etc.

Daffodil: Bulb. S & C. Pinch off at base of flower at point where it joins the stem. Discard stems; wires can be added later. Insert the tubular base of the daffodil into the medium (silica gel or other material) which should be about two inches deep. The petals should rest flat on top and the cup will be upright. Gently sift medium over the petals and build it around the cup. Lastly, fill the cup and completely but lightly cover the entire flower. As the daffodils are extremely fragile, great care must be taken in removing them from the medium after they are dry. Use a small paintbrush to push aside part of this that the flower may be lifted out without tearing. Some daffodils dry more successfully than others (examples: "Beersheba" and "Fortune"). Experiment with the different varieties that you have. Silica gel recommended. Face up.

Dahlia: Annual or tuber. S & C. Silica gel recommended. Face up.

Delphinium: Perennial. S & C. Dry individual florets, face up, (wiring first) or whole spike, horizontal. Light blue is lovely.

Dock: Field flower. Cut when green or reddish. Hang or dry in upright position for graceful curves.

Dogwood: Tree. S & C. Protect from summer humidity. Face up or down. Check state conservation regulation on use.

Feverfew: Perennial. S & C. Dry white varieties over heat to retain whiteness of petals. Silica gel recommended. Face down.

Gladiolus: Bulb. S & C. Silica gel (face up) for individual blossoms wired first for substitute stems. Horizontal for spikes. We recommend drying partial spikes as we consider entire stalks impractical. This flower is extremely delicate being easily affected by the slightest touch of humidity. We recommend with reservations the drying of gladiolus.

Globe Amaranth: Annual. H. Easily dried.

Globe Thistle: Perennial. H. Cut when green or just after the first tinge of blue shows *before* buds open.

Goldenrod: Field flower. H. Gather when about three-fourths of the florets have opened. It is important to cut at the right time. There are many varieties; if early blooming ones are missed, look for others later.

Gloriosa Daisy: Perennial. S & C. Face down.

Hollyhock: Perennial. S & C. Exceptionally lovely. Single blooms are easily dried *face-down.* Insert *short piece of wire in pinched-off* bloom (longer wire or florist pick stem can be added later). Make a small mound of cotton and fit flower over this. Then barely cover petals with medium. Dry double hollyhocks *face-up.*

Hydrangea, Blue: [Hydrangea hortensis] Shrub. H. Valuable for its color.

Hydrangea: [Hydrangea paniculata grandiflora] Shrub. H. Cut flowers *after* they have fully matured when green or rose-pink. Green, especially desirable. The larger flower heads may be divided into smaller clusters for use in arrangements.

Joe-Pye Weed: Field flower. H. Cut when buds have reached height of color but before they begin to open.

Knotweed: [Polygonum] Weedy shrub. H. Cut when it turns crimson.

Larkspur: Annual. All colors. Very valuable, especially double varieties. Dries easily by hanging, especially desirable if dried horizontally. S & C.

Marigold: Annual. S & C. Clear yellow and orange varieties. R: "Man-in-the-Moon," "Lemon Drop." Face up or down.

Mexican Sunflower: [Tithonia] Annual. S & C. Must be cut as soon as flower matures, or petals will fall. Face down.

Pansy and Viola: Annual. S & C. Face up.

Pearly Everlasting or Immortelle: Field flower. H. Gather just *before* buds begin to open.

Orchid: Perennial. S & C. Silica gel recommended. Cattleyas dry well and last well.

Peony: Perennial: S & C. Double varieties—clear pink and crimson dry better than white. Japanese varieties—white and all colors—especially desirable.

Phlox: Annual or perennial. S & C. Silica gel recommended.

Pussy Willow: Shrub H. Cut when catkins are well formed. Branches may be tied into graceful curves. After four or five days they may be used either with dried flowers or in water with fresh flowers.

Queen Anne's Lace: Field flower. S & C. Gather early in season when flowers are large. Face down. Stems will be stiff at first but will bend during drying if not supported. To hold them in upright position, after flower heads have been covered with medium lattice–work top of box with string drawn through slits.

Rose: Shrub. H. or S & C. Attractive when dried hanging, though edges will curl. For a more natural effect, dry *face-up* by S & C. method. Silica gel recommended. Cut when in bud or partly open. R: Hybrid tea "Charlotte Armstrong," grandiflora "Queen Elizabeth," floribunda "Floradora." Dry small cluster roses *face-down* with stems in upright position, uncovered. R: Polyantha "The Fairy."

Statice: Annual. H. All colors good; white very pure. Extremely valuable flower.

Strawflower: Annual. H. Pick when buds are one third open. Each flower, as soon as it blooms, may be pinched from stem and put on heavy florist wire, but most effective when used in arrangements if clusters of the flowers, cut with their own stems are made by binding together with Scotch tape. This will reinforce them as stems are very brittle. Break stems off below the tape and, with very fine wire, fasten to a florist wire to use as a substitute.

Snow-on-the-Mountain: [Euphorbia] Annual. Sows itself prolifically. Very attractive but take care not to get milky juice in eyes, mouth or cuts. S. & C.

Verbena: Annual. S & C. Silica gel recommended. Face down.

Yarrow: [Achillea] Perennial. H. Yellow varieties especially good. R: "Gold Plate."

Veronica: Perennial S & C. (R) "Icicle."

Zinnia: Zinnia Annual. S & C. Clear colors dry best.

foliage

Artemesia: Perennial. H. R.: "Silver King." Provides lovely silvery-gray foliage. Cut in fall when tiny inconspicuous flowers are in bloom.

Beech: [Fagus grandiflora] Tree. Most useful, either green or with autumn coloring of gold. Glycerin solution.

Boxwood: Shrub. Very attractive. Golden yellow when dried in glycerin solution.

Eucalyptus: H. small-leaved varieties. Can be bought at florist shops.

Ferns: (R) "Christmas" and "Maidenhair." Press between pages of magazines.

Honeysuckle: (winter) (R) "*Lonicera Fragrantissima.*

Ivy Leaves: Soak in glycerin solution.

Magnolia Grandiflora: Tree. When dried between magazine pages but *not* weighted, leaves will be a pretty shade of silver-green and with florist picks attached these can be used in arrangements and are most attractive. When branches are treated in glycerin solution the leaves turn a lovely brown.

Maple, Red: Tree. Leaves with fall coloring are good source of red for arrangements. Press.

Mullein: Field flower. Foliage is a lovely soft green. Dry rosettes. S & C. Face up.

Periwinkle or Trailing Myrtle: [Vinca Minor] S & C.

Salal: From Canada and Alaska. Can be bought at florists. Soft light green. S & C.

Scotch Broom: H. Wrap with soft wire for desired curves.

Sumac: Shrub. Red foliage dried in autumn will retain red coloring. Be *sure* to cut when first turns red or leaves will drop. Press between pages of magazines.

seed pods, berries, and grasses

These add interest and variety to dried arrangements. Many beautiful pods, berries, and grasses which do not grow in your locality may be purchased from the florist.

berries (h. for all)

Bittersweet: Vine. Follow state conservation restrictions.

Bush Cranberry: Shrub.

Blackberry Lily: Perennial.

Nandina: Shrub.
Privet: Berries may be dried when green or dark blue. R: "Amur River" and broad-leaved evergreen variety "Ligustrum Lucidum."
Sumac: Shrub. Cut when fruit heads are green or when they first turn red.
Violet Jewel Berry: [Callicarpa purpurea] Shrub.

seed pods (h. for all)

Chinese Lantern: Perennial. Pods dry orange-red.
Hardy Blue Spirea: [Caryopteris] Shrub. Cut as soon as small blue florets have fallen. Dries a lovely soft green. Very effective and useful.
Honesty or Money Plant: [Lunaria annua] Biennial. When pod is dry, carefully peel off outside layers.
Milkweed: Field flower. Cut pod when green, as soon as it is fully formed. Allow about four or five weeks to dry; then press open and remove seeds. Bend pod back to force it to remain open, revealing beautiful yellow lining.
Poppy: Perennial. Cut when green.
Yucca: Perennial. Cut when green, will turn yellow.

For stunning yellow-green, cut hazel-nut branches with nuts in green cases. They will be ready to cut sometime during July.

grasses and other materials (h. for all)

Bearded Barley, Cat-tail, Corn Tassels, Marsh Grass, Peppergrass, Quakergrass, Sea-oats, Sugar Cane, etc.

storing dried flowers

Flowers should always be stored in a dry place. Keep them in darkness until they are ready to be used in arrangements, since light tends to fade them. It is an easy matter to store flowers that have been dried by the hanging method. They may be left hanging, kept in boxes or put in any convenient place until ready to be used.

There is more of a problem with flowers dried by the Surrounding and Covering Method since summer humidity is inclined to cause their petals to droop and crumple. If you live in a very dry climate, or have an air-conditioning system that runs constantly, you will have no difficulty whatsoever; if not, then some special means must be devised to protect them until the furnace is on in the fall.

A satisfactory way is to store them in a closet in which is hung a large bag of absorbent clay impregnated with calcium chloride (De-Moist). Check as directed, to determine when maximum moisture is absorbed and it is ready for reactivation. The flowers may be hung, placed upright in Styrofoam or tumblers, or their heads may be put flat on hardware cloth that has been placed over cartons, allowing the stem to hang through the mesh. Take care that heads of the flowers do not touch while being stored.

If no closet is available stand flowers in inch thick Styrofoam, cut to fit inside of a carton without a top, containing a small bag of De-Moist. Cover carton over all with a large plastic bag such as those in which cleaners hang dresses. To be certain that no air will get into the box twist both ends of the bag very tightly and secure with an elastic band. Check two or three times during the summer and reactivate the dehumidifying agent accordingly.

Daffodils and other very short stemmed flowers may be placed upon a piece of hardware cloth that has been propped in a shallow box or carton containing De-Moist; with the airtight plastic over them they can be watched all during the summer and early fall.

steaming the flowers

If, in spite of all precautions, some of the flowers become bent or twisted they may often be restored to their original shape by being held over steam from a tea kettle and quickly smoothed into place. They will again become dry, especially if this is done after the heat has been turned on in the fall. For extra precaution select a sunny day when the humidity is low.

life of a dried flower

We have found that the length of time that a dried flower will last does not depend upon the method nor the medium used for dehydration, but upon the composition and texture of the flower itself. Cockscomb and strawflowers may be used in arrangements for several years while most of the others will begin to fade after one season. We prefer to make new dried arrangements every fall.

making dried arrangements

In making dried arrangements, use the same principle that you use in working with fresh material, the only difference being that because of shrinkage, you will need more dried than fresh flowers.

For a line or a mass arrangement, first establish the line or outline. Next, place large flowers, or flower clusters, towards the front as a focal point and then fill in the space between, choosing materials of different interesting shapes and harmonious colors. Allow several leaves and some flowers and other material to extend over the front edge of the container so that its line will be broken.

If the container with which you are working is shallow, or if it is bowl-shaped, use *dry* Oasis to serve as a flower holder. It may be secured in this manner; put two-inch *roofing nails* through plastic adhesive tape two inches in length, adhere to bottom of container and press Oasis on points. Two or more nails will be needed for each arrangement. A large lump of flower-arranging clay can also be used as a holder in a shallow bowl.

Other types of containers may be filled with sand. Moistening this slightly will facilitate holding the flowers in place while working with them, and after the arrangement is completed and the sand has hardened, they will, *if undisturbed,* never move. We also highly recommend using Oasis for deep containers, as well as for shallow, especially if it can be cut to fit and left slightly above the rim. By doing this the flowers can easily be put in at all angles.

We are indebted to Eleanor Reed Bolton (author and lecturer) for still another method of holding dried flowers in a container when making an arrangement. It is to fit a piece of green Styrofoam, half inch thick, into the top and place some flower-arranging clay that has been shaped into pancake form over the Styrofoam, pressing it firmly to the sides of the container. This technique is especially advantageous when arrangements are made in glass as, of course, there will be no unsightly stems to show, but can be used only when containers are slightly flaring at the top.

In making dried arrangements, wires in several degrees of thickness are very useful. Use these for extending stems and bending flowers or branches in curving lines. If the wires show, they can be given a more naturalistic look by being covered with florist tape that is stretched and wound spirally around the wires. Florist picks, all sizes, paraffin, toothpicks, Scotch and florist tape (use to reinforce brittle stems), will also be helpful. Sometimes a fallen petal can be replaced with a bit of glue; a broken petal may be patched with Scotch tape. Another useful accessory to have on hand will be a supply of extra lengths of hollow stems (example, larkspur). A heavy florist wire will fit into them. You will find this especially helpful in working with such flowers as hollyhocks and daffodils.

When the arrangements are finished to your entire satisfaction and placed in their permanent positions, you will find that beauty, charm and distinction have been added to your home. The gaily colored and pastel flowers will be enjoyed by your family, admired by your friends and best of all, will last all winter.

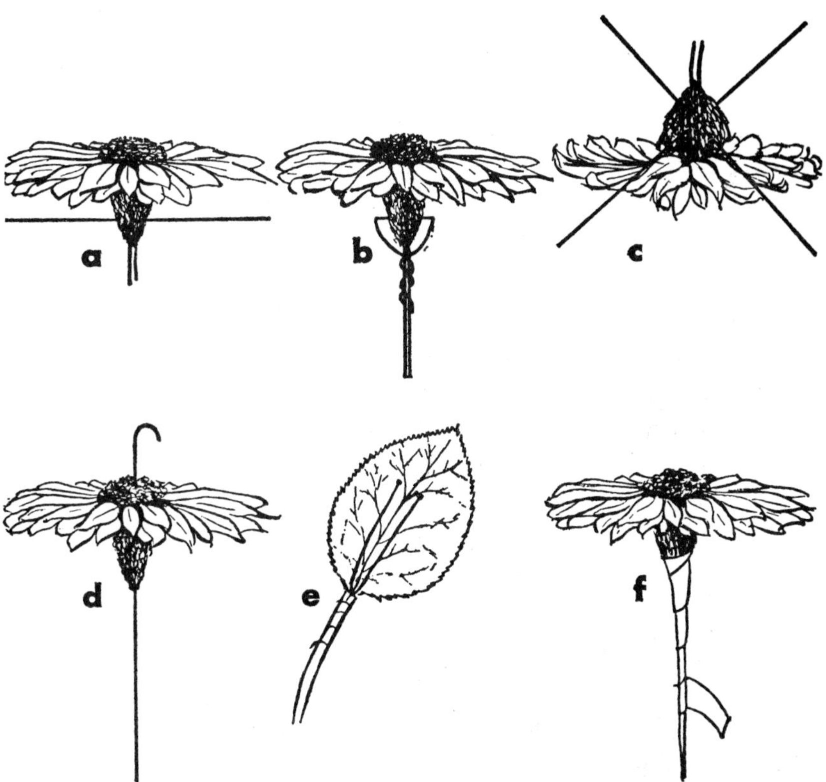

Making substitute stems. a) Insert florist wire through calyx; b) twist to tighten; c) heavier flowers may need cross pieces of wire which are then twisted together to make a stem; d) hook method of wiring for flowers such as hollyhocks that are pinched from the stalk; e) wiring leaves to make substitute stems; f) conceal with florist tape any wires which will show in finished arrangement.

index